Why Not Take a Second Look?

by

Yvette I. Stanford-Scotland

DORRANCE PUBLISHING CO
EST. 1920
PITTSBURGH, PENNSYLVANIA 15238

Dorrance Publishing Co
585 Alpha Drive
Suite 103
Pittsburgh, PA 15238
Visit our website at *www.dorrancebookstore.com*

ISBN: 979-8-88925-995-4
eISBN: 978-1-6376-4626-7

Firstly, I want to thank God for the privilege of enabling me to pen poetry in His name and honor.

Secondly, I would like to extend my heartfelt appreciation to my younger sibling, Pamela Stanford-Odle, for her patience and encouragement along this journey. Thanks for all your assistance.

Next, to Sister Darnel Atkinson who has been a source of inspiration and encouragement throughout this process. Thanks for praying for its publishing.

Lastly, but certainly not the least, I want to say a heartfelt thank you to my husband, Leroy Scotland, and children, Shawn and Sherece, for their support.

All praise and glory is given to God.

Contents

Why Not Take a Second Look?

The Majesty of God

The majesty of God always amazes me
As in nature I intently search for thee.
Astounding displays of your creative power
Force me to my knees, and I often cower.

Everywhere my eyes behold your ingenious power
The inexplicable heavens display the grandeur.
Revolving planets, galaxies with billions of stars
Cascading, never colliding, never involved in wars.

The trees in Fall, without human intervention
Shed colorful foliage, trusting thy protection,
That in Spring they'll fruit after they blossom,
And be clothed with leaves from top to bottom.

From country to country each and every year,
Birds navigate the pathless sky under your care;
Migrating birds from thousands of miles away,
Pass tiny Monarch Butterflies silently on their way.

Moon, galaxies and stars each night exclaim,
There is a God; the beating heart proclaims,
He guides the blood through miles of veins,
God is our Creator; He all boundaries frame.

Tongue cannot amply tell, nor mind perceive,
The goodness of God in whom I firmly believe.
My heart is overwhelmed; I now truly confess,
For God to redeem man; we're eternally blessed.

Storms of Life

Ominous black clouds suddenly overshadowed the sky,
They seem so angry, and I'm nervously wondering why?
The forecast had predicted the day would be clear,
But right now, there are angry storm clouds everywhere.

The swiftly moving storm my safety now threatens
As the thick, turbulent gray clouds gather and thicken.
Believing the forecast would be correct as predicted
For rain I didn't prepare; my raingear I had restricted.

It seems as though I will be caught in the deluge
With no place in sight where I can seek quick refuge.
The approaching storm fills me with anxious forebodings,
Lord, I need shelter, while the clouds, the rain is holding.

My thoughts, like the clouds, are scurrying around my head
What should I do? What path can I this late moment tread?
To escape this approaching, gloomy, impending storm,
That from a clear, cloudless sky was suddenly born.

Oftentimes in life we find ourselves totally unprepared,
For those Summer downspouts that are fast but rear.
But we don't have to panic if suddenly caught within,
For Jesus provides shelter from both storms and sin.

The storm reaffirms my faith; Jesus will come someday,
And the skies will never again angry, storm clouds display.
All will be peace with Jesus, the infinite source of our light
No more fears or foreboding, for all will be joy and delight.

So, the next time you see the sky beginning to darken
Remember Jesus, your Savior, still controls the heaven.
He controls the shifting clouds, the wind and the rain,
He cares for you; He never ever wants to cause you pain.

My Life Down Here

Often, I think I'm endowed with the necessary tools,
To carve out my life; pay no attention to God's rules.
I have a sound education which affords me good pay,
Good friends to support me, whether at work or play.

So far I've done very well, I'm almost at the top!
There seems to be no reason now why I should stop.
Lately, a voice seems to be competing for my attention
Pleading incessantly with a deep, soul-searching question.

My dear, what is your mission and real life's goal?
Where are you going to end after this grand stroll?
This brief life here on earth is not your final end,
Remember, you'll meet Jesus either as judge or friend!

To be quite honest, I hadn't given it much thought,
I was more interested in the sales of the stuff I bought.
Ensuring I was the winner in every endeavor I undertook,
No more thought of God once the church I forsook!

I was tempted to think I was here on my own,
And totally forgot that my life here was on loan.
There's a God to whom I must render a faithful account,
Of all things I have done; even ones I neglected to count.

The fallacy of a "good" education made me falsely believe,
I was doing well because of the many accolades I received.
I despised the Ten Commandments and neglected to pray,
And very late realized I had strayed far from the true way.

This old battered, worn-out body I consent to surrender,
Please, accept me, Dear Jesus; forgive my many blunders.
You are the potter, I have no elaborate design or plan
My life I fully surrender, my life is now in Your hand.

The Christian Race

When I started upon this Christian race
I never imagined the hardships I would face.
The battle proved to be terribly fierce.
Satan relentlessly tried my heart to pierce.

From morn till night deadly darts were hurled;
New trials constantly, daily unfurled.
But God, His promises did wonderfully keep,
He never once deserted this erring sheep.

Daily I rise and to my dear Savior repair
To seek protection, learn how not to fear.
His words I study, His commandments I obey
Even though I often stumble along the way.

This cunning foe I cannot hope to defeat,
If I become careless, waste time, don't keep,
The laws God has given to me as a guide;
For obeying them keeps God by my side.

The promises of God help me to focus be
To continue the race when the end I can't see.
The road is rough, the struggles bitter and long,
But Jesus has in my troubled heart placed a song.

Safe from all harm, though battered and sore,
Soon this perilous journey will at last be ore.
By God's grace I'll safely reach the other shore,
There sweet Jesus I'll meet to part nevermore.

Presumption

Why is everyone constantly preaching to me?
When I have decided exactly what I desire to be.
I will live my life in a manner well pleasing to me,
Stop badgering and sermonizing; just let me be.

Now a sinner by choice, I lived as I well pleased,
And soon my conscience was also put at eased.
In rebellion I boldly stepped onto the highway of pride,
Caring not if I survived, or in pursuing pleasure, I died.

Lofty morals which once characterized my Christian life,
Were slowly replaced with drunkenness and strife.
Still my sinful, stubborn will refused to bow or bend
I'd made my choice; determined where, how, and when.

Sorely tempted and tried, I frequently succumbed,
To many temptations that I had previously overcome.
Life and hope spiraled downward into decadence and sin,
Behavior once thought unimaginable, I now relished within.

Then someone stepped in and a total change was wrought,
It was Jesus, and for my degenerate life He gallantly fought.
Never leaving, though I oft drifted back and forth into sin,
He stayed, as promised, daily battling the demons within.

"The wages of sin is death," I've often times been told,
But the horrors accompanying sin is dreadful to behold!
From God's precepts I will never again presumptuously drift,
For in sin's swelling tide, one loses grip and is soon set adrift.

The Fire Cannot Come
Where the Fire Has Already Been!

My home is stretched out on the prairie wide,
There are miles of grassland on every side.
Our farm provides, but the work is backbreaking
Thank God for each hand who has been hardworking.

The sunrise and sunset regulate our hectic lives,
All hands are on deck; servants, children, and wife,
Must cook, clean, wash and often the fields plow,
Thank God each one knows when, where, and how.

The good days were threatened one late summer morn,
When a strong wind from the East was suddenly born.
There's something unusual about this wind, can you tell?
Oh no, there's smoke; the prairie has turned to hell.

"Quick, boys, the raging fire is swiftly coming this way,
We must work hard and fast and continue to pray."
Firebreaks are the only way to stop this raging fire,
All hands on deck; call all whom we can quickly hire.

Let's burn a wide patch around the house and barn,
Make it big enough so that we'll be safe from harm.
The leaping, advancing flames are terrifying to behold,
Would this fire devour all, or would the firebreak hold?

In terror and disbelief, we watched and fervently prayed,
As the flames danced higher, advanced, and cinders spayed.
Please, Lord, save our lives, homes and farms tonight!
We've done all we can this consuming fire to fight.

The fast-burning fire soon arrived at the place
Where we created the wide firebreaks in haste.
The conflagration shot upward then suddenly stopped,
The firebreak was too wide for the raging fire to hop.

"What happened, Dad?" his son asked with voice so keen,
"The fire cannot come, where the fire has already been."
The firebreak has held; we are now safe from all harm
God brought relief, thanks to Him for saving our farm.

The firebreak held at Calvary when Jesus died on the Cross,
Satan no longer has any claim; he's no longer the boss.
If you come now to Jesus, you will most certainly find,
The Cross, God's firebreak, has power to hold Satan's line.

The Warring Elements!

Some thick gray clouds marshalled themselves in the eastern sky
Readied themselves for battle with a portion of the earth nearby.
The wind entered the fray and presumed to blow them away,
There'll be no storms or thunderstorms; no deluge here today.

The clouds grew angry and in fury beckoned to some others,
Join the brigade, we will with clouds assuage; with wind don't bother.
Soon clouds built up stretching from the bottom to the very top
Now let wind assail, see if it has the power this storm to stop.

What a sight to behold, the warring elements waged a pounding toll
Upon each other; as militant winds tossed storm clouds like a scroll.
The precocious winds firmly blockade the path of the pursuing clouds;
Then earth, with prejudice, cheered the clapping of thunder loud.

With poignant feelings I silently stood and observed them both
Needing water but fearing floods and debris would certainly choke,
The waterways bringing death and destruction in their wake.
Oh, clouds, stop amassing, disperse, be brisk for earth's sake.

Sun watched as the heavenly elements battled for supremacy,
Determined that neither would gain it; just you wait and see.
I have preeminence, I'll burn storm clouds, let them dissipate, disappear,
Leave a manageable few to water the earth in that corner over there.

The battles in life may resemble the elements struggling for mastery,
Each emotion striving for ascendency; dictating with pride and lunacy.
But thanks be to God, when we pray, the devil and his demons flee,
When to Jesus we turn; He the storm clouds dissipates, setting us free.

The Wind

It was a nice day and the wind was at play
Dancing with the trees as they bobbed and swayed.
When to the canopy my eyes were suddenly drawn,
A strong gust of wind bent the branches, revealing the dawn.

Then higher up my gaze at last reached the cloudy sky,
Where white clouds formations were swiftly floating by.
Scarcely could I recognize a figure before it was disfigured,
Fleeting as the moments were these shapely, cloudy figures.

Blowing through the trees, the wind rustling sounds produced
As the leaves danced, the wind new chorography introduced.
Sudden variation in speed, bent the canopy this way and that
Now a sudden gust of wind is dancing with my summer hat.

Each shift and turn the wind a new shape in the sky created,
Briefly there admired, but soon no longer well delineated.
While gazing at the beauty fleetingly displayed for admiration,
My thoughts drifted beyond the clouds to the God of creation.

My thoughts are racing, randomly, as the floating clouds above,
Transient are pictures formed about God's never-ending love.
How can I with lasting stability of character anchor myself?
From shifting winds of doctrines as they present themselves.

Let the word of God my firm anchor in this world be,
Let my thoughts and passions be focused Lord on thee.
Winds of doctrines will blow, shift and often change,
May I stand firm, rejecting every doctrine that is strange.

Too Late for Mending Holes

The farmer's wife nervously looked out at the enticing hole,
Did John mend that fence? Did he do as he was told?
The sheep often graze near the green pasture nearby,
I don't want the lamb the hole in the fence to spy.

The mother sheep soon noticed the little lamb was gone,
He'd strayed from the pasture and gone far beyond,
The reach of his mother and the procrastinating farmer,
Exposed to dangers as he around the fields wandered.

The farmer looked long and hard but there was no sound,
Neither wool nor skin from the lamb was anywhere found.
With deep regret the farmer patched the broken fence,
Wishing he'd listened to his wife; now he was tensed.

Whose fault was it that the innocent lamb was lost?
Was it the farmer who procrastinated; at what cost?
Was it the innocent lamb who knew not the boundaries?
Or the farmer's wife who for weeks voiced her worries?

It matters not to whom the blame for the lost is ascribed.
The lamb's hopelessly lost, it's no longer by its mother's side.
Irreversible damage was done to all who lived on the farm,
The poor creature had come to sudden and complete harm.

Certain steps must immediately be taken to secure the rest.
We can't afford another tragedy; each must do his very best.
Mending fences after lambs are gone only amplifies the harm,
'Tis a very unwise way to raise sheep and lambs on a farm.

Many parents wait until the child is fixed in his impious ways,
Then unsuccessfully try to curb desires leading them astray.
An older tree is more likely under pressure to break than bend,
Begin while young; ensure the holes in the fence you mend.

Frustration in the Garden

My knowledge of farmland and soil was zero,
When it came to zeal, I could be deemed a hero.
I meant it when I vowed to keep it free from weeds,
Planning to wage a war of terror on them indeed.

By now you've guessed I intended to plant a garden,
The best that could be found, and I would be the warden.
There would be neat beds of vegetables of every kind.
Which nowhere else in the neighborhood you could find.

Each morning the ground I attacked with zest and zeal,
Certain such efforts a bountiful crop the garden would yield,
An abundance of everything planted, molded and watered,
Soon there'll be copious showers; the garden cannot falter.

To my surprise saplings sprouted where I had not planted,
Growing much faster than the seeds I had carefully potted.
In every space and between the tender germinating seeds,
A profusion of every kind of the wretched, worthless weeds.

I pulled and weeded, then pulled some more and more
Certain I could rid the garden of weeds; I became sore.
The neighbors I consulted, the local farmers I visited,
"Learn how to be free from the pesky weeds," I insisted.

A game soon developed as the weeds circumvented,
Efforts to eradicate them; even new methods invented.
So obsessed was I of ridding the garden of annoying weeds,
Much time was stolen from tending the plants we did need.

It dawned on me mental commitment and arduous works,
Were insufficient to eradicate weeds or a habit that hurts.
Man cannot with rigorous works rid himself of evil and sin
Only with Jesus and the Holy Spirit's power can man ever win.

The Body Speaks

My body early this morning sent a stern warning to me,
I need from sugar, oils, and saturated fats to be freed.
No longer can I tolerate the garbage that's included
In my daily diet; it's time all junk food is precluded.

The head to the indulgent palate delivered a strong rebuke,
"You're not in charge of this body, that belief is a fluke."
The mind will determine the choices from this day forward,
A nutritious diet is a must, there's no going backward.

A meeting was conducted to all the internal organs' delight,
For they longed to bring to light their unseen, arduous plight.
The stress and the strain caused by the lack of proper food
Was injurious to health; they couldn't regulate the mood.

Another complaint the stomach cited at the council,
Was the uncertainty and irregularity of meals, it whistled.
Somedays breakfast was served in the morning at nine,
Other days nothing was provided; the stomach repined.

Why can't the body be informed of the agreed sleeping time?
When activities will cease; little rest and no recovery isn't fine.
One cannot continue to function like a galloping horse all day,
Time must be allotted for rest, meditation, and meaningful play.

The feet were annoyed at their treatment and bitterly complained,
The body was "wearing them out"; gladly was the motion sustained.
From such painful behaviors please desist; feet also brought to light
"Proper fitting shoes were needed; too often the fancy ones were
tight."

The center of learning, the head, was ordered a nutrition class to take,
If peradventure habits will improve for the impoverished body's sake.
A balance diet must be daily prepared involving head, hands and eyes,
They too must be involved; sometimes they felt totally despised.

A new concept was purported about the different food groups,
The plate must have a representation of each, even when it's soup.
Too often the choice of food was left to the enterprising eyes,
Selected based on sight alone; nutritious value was not prized.

A time was assigned for the audacious changes to be implemented,
The body must be nourished; and every part readily complimented.
A holistic approach to life is now part of the body's world view,
Fruits and vegetables must be incorporated, they are long overdue.

The Sea and the Seashore

Standing on the beach gazing at the waves one sunny afternoon,
I watched the frothing waves crest on the shore and swooned.
In the path of the incoming tide lay rocks of all sizes and shapes,
Diverting the water around and over them, providing a way of escape.

Just how long had the boulders and rocks occupied that very space?
How long they'd been immovable, unperturbed by the crashing waves.
The unobtrusive conflict waging between the boulders and the sea
Must have begun centuries ago; both were as formidable as can be.

The swirling tides smashed sand and stones twice daily over the rocks,
Scouring their faces as they crashed over the mighty, majestic blocks.
For so long the rocks had been contending with the returning waves,
Do they ever get tired? Do they ever some really peaceful days crave?

This daily conflict must have brought some permanent changes,
The severity of which depends on how unyielding the tide rages.
What exactly was changing at the juncture was very hard to tell,
The indiscernible changes were measured only by the breaking swells.

The smoothness of the rocks testified to the lengthy encountered,
Between the sea and its allies; the winds, the waves, the boulder
The slow grind of the sand over time pressed and rounded the curves,
Making changes randomly as sand, waves and stones all converged.

So too the annoyances in our lives our character slowly does build,
Removing sin and dross, cutting and chiseling, yet needing more still.
The rocks on the shore never complain as the rough sea waves return,
Washing makes them clean they know, especially after being sun burned.

Conflict between Eye and Stomach

As I sat down some food to eat
Providing relief for my sore feet,
I attacked a large plate of food;
Instantly I was in a good mood.

The food to the eye was pleasing,
But to the stomach was destressing.
The fat will my many arteries clog,
The sweets will put me in a fog.

My palate the plate sorely defended,
It's colorful enough, be contented.
The food groups are all represented,
Eat without being so offended.

It's nice to hear from you, my friend,
But digestion doesn't upon you depend.
The stomach has the food to process,
Kidney and liver are loaded with excess.

Can't some agreement be reached
About the food requested by each.
'Tis time the brain take full control,
Of meals that down the shoot are doled.

The body must operate as a whole,
No individual part will decisions mold.
Benefits must be received by all
No food exceptions allowed at all.

Devoted Like Mary

Oh, to be like Mary after her conversion,
Displaying the same loyalty and devotion.
To have one and only one heavenly goal
To dedicate my life, my heart, my soul.

You don't understand the burdens I once carried
Tormented by sin and guilt, I was always harried.
Dragged into the presence of the Holy Teacher
My head I bowed; fearful to face the preacher.

Today's my last; soon by this mob I will be stoned,
By the very ones who tempted; now I'm all alone.
My sins are great; who would save a wretch like me?
Is it too late for this sinner to come to thee?

Strange! the Master is writing messages in the sand
Never has a verdict been written by Jesus' hand.
It's my fault, there's really no one else to blame
My secret sins will be publicly read; oh, the shame!

From the corner of my eyes feet quickly shuffle past;
What stirred their pretentious hearts? Why walk so fast?
Convicted by the one from whom they sought a conviction
Men quietly fled, lest all discover their horrid pretentions.

Forsaken by my accusers; with stones dropped nearby,
To the conceited mob Jesus gave no answer, no reply.
 "Neither do I condemn you, go and sin no more."
Jesus that day forgave me, of that I am totally sure.

Don't think my devotion strange; Jesus saved me,
When others clamored for my life; He set free.
I'll work for Him as long as I shall on this earth live,
Everything I have, or own, to Him I'll gratefully give.

'Tis my joy, my honor to wash my Savior's feet,
My hair's a poor substitute for drying; I weep,
He granted me permission at the feast to serve
In his mission on earth; such goodness I didn't deserve.

www.ingramcontent.com/pod-product-compliance
Lightning Source LLC
Chambersburg PA
CBHW040901110726
48005CB00001B/158